Reptile Poems

Compiled by John Foster

Contents

The lizard *Tony Mitton* 2
Step by step *Gina Douthwaite* 4
The watching crocodile *Irene Rawnsley* 6
The giant tortoise *Richard James* 8
Snake *Angi Holden* 12
Meeting the snake *Tony Mitton* 14
Our dragon *Wendy Larmont* 16

Acknowledgements

The Editor and Publisher wish to thank the following who have kindly given permission for the use of copyright material:

Gina Douthwaite for 'Step by step' © 1996 Gina Douthwaite; Angi Holden for 'Snake' © 1996 Angi Holden; Richard James for 'The giant tortoise' © 1996 Richard James; Wendy Larmont for 'Our dragon' © 1996 Wendy Larmont; Tony Mitton for 'Meeting the snake' and 'The lizard' both © 1996 Tony Mitton; Irene Rawnsley for 'The watching crocodile' © 1996 Irene Rawnsley.

The lizard

'There are no dragons,'
my father said.
'What's more, the dinosaurs
are dead.'

But just today,
on a warm stone wall,
I saw a dragon,
swift and small.

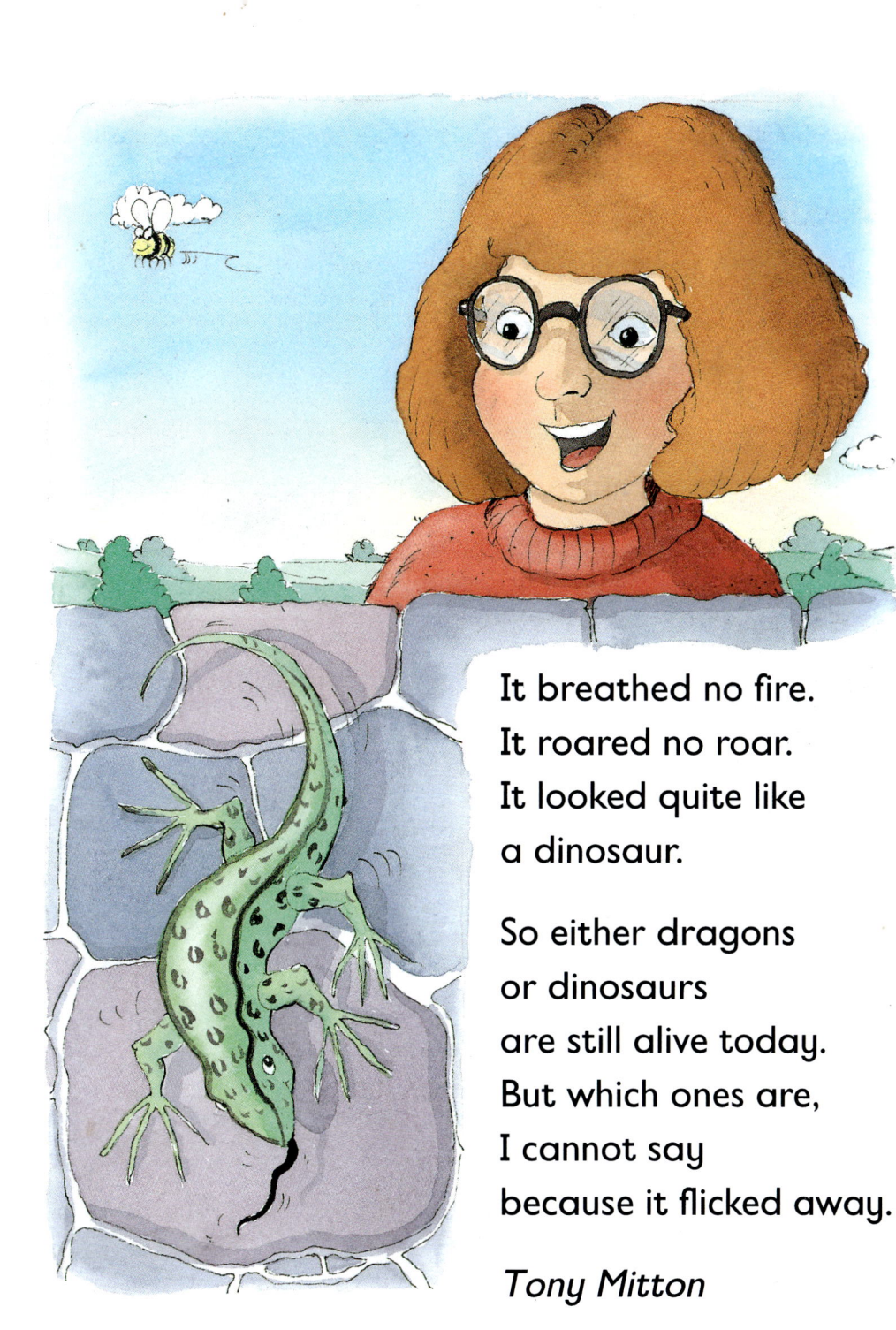

It breathed no fire.
It roared no roar.
It looked quite like
a dinosaur.

So either dragons
or dinosaurs
are still alive today.
But which ones are,
I cannot say
because it flicked away.

Tony Mitton

Step by step

Long time ago
a fish grew feet;

walked upon the land,
couldn't stand the heat;

got a thicker skin
of horny scales;

looked more like a dinosaur
with long toe-nails;

laid a batch of eggs,
hatched baby crocodiles.

From fish long ago
came today's reptiles.

Gina Douthwaite

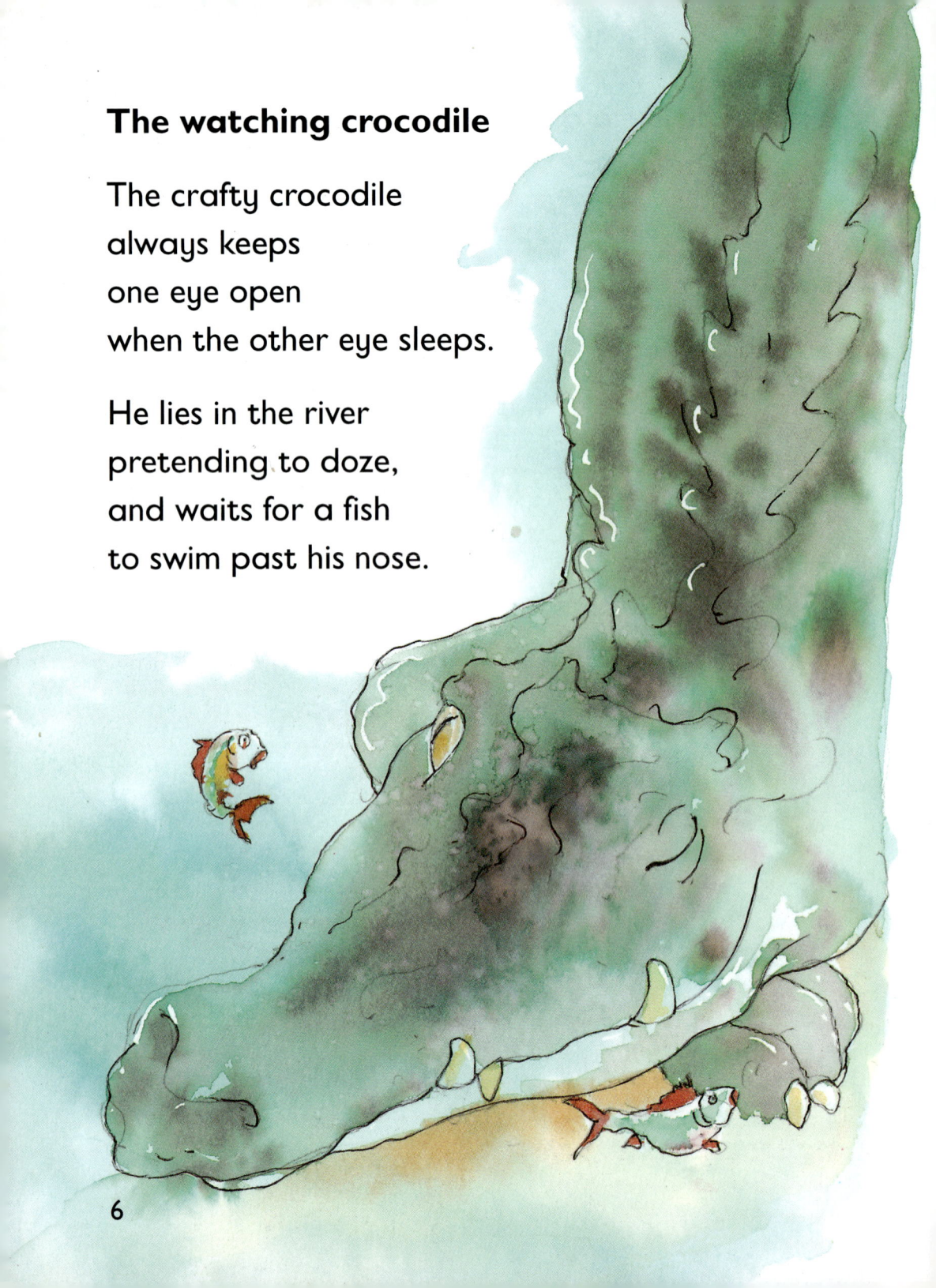

The watching crocodile

The crafty crocodile
always keeps
one eye open
when the other eye sleeps.

He lies in the river
pretending to doze,
and waits for a fish
to swim past his nose.

Snap! go his jaws;
the meal is gone.
He smiles and waits
for another one.

Take care, little fishes
as you swim by.
Remember, remember
the crocodile's eye.

Irene Rawnsley

The giant tortoise

It stretched out its neck
And it started to crawl.
It crawled through a fence
And it crawled through a wall.

When the giant tortoise moves
Nothing can stop it.

It crawled past the lions
And the kangaroo.
It crawled through a gate
And escaped from the zoo.

When the giant tortoise moves
Nothing can stop it.

It crawled up the road.
It crawled into town.
It knocked three lamps
And a pillar box down.

When the giant tortoise moves
Nothing can stop it.

It flattened a policeman.
It flattened a tree.
What will it flatten next?
Don't ask me!

When the giant tortoise moves
Nothing can stop it.

Richard James

Snake

Shiny
snake,
skin
shimmering,
slip-
sliding
silently,
spies
sleepy
spider
spinning
soft
silken
strands
— snap,
supper.

Angi Holden

13

Meeting the snake

I used to fear you,
slithery snake,
the way you move,
the shapes you make.

But now I've met you
at the zoo,
I've changed the way
I think of you.

I used to think you
slippy, sly.
And yet I find you
clean and dry,

and soft and slow
and good to touch.
So now I do not fear you,
much.

Tony Mitton

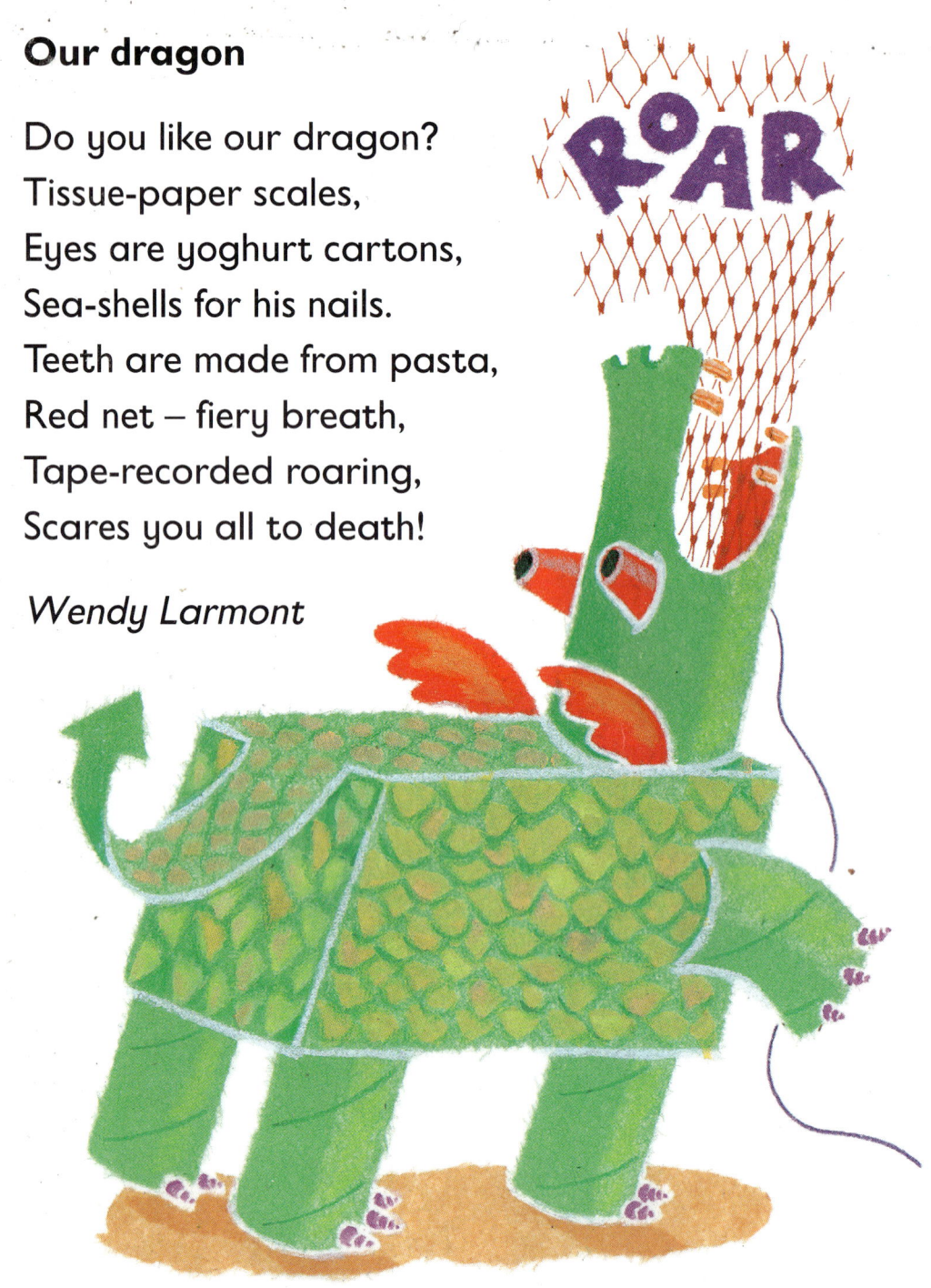

Our dragon

Do you like our dragon?
Tissue-paper scales,
Eyes are yoghurt cartons,
Sea-shells for his nails.
Teeth are made from pasta,
Red net – fiery breath,
Tape-recorded roaring,
Scares you all to death!

Wendy Larmont